Offline-First Applications
Synchronize Effectively, Always

Table of Contents

Chapter 1. Introduction

In a digital world that is ever-critical of application performance, Offline-First Applications have emerged as a pivotal toolset. Our Special Report delves into the nuanced landscape of these applications, focusing on the crucial aspect of effective synchronization. Even for readers with little technical background, our report illuminates this powerful concept in a down-to-earth and approachable manner. We invite you to journey with us as we explore the design, development, and deployment of these applications. Discover how they ensure seamless service delivery, irrespective of connectivity concerns, and comprehend how pivotal they could be in your digital evolution. This Report is a trove of insights and practical strategies, so whether you're an industry professional, a tech enthusiast, or a curious novice, there's something of high value waiting for you.

Chapter 2. Understanding the Offline-First Approach

In the ever-changing world of technology, 'Offline-First' is a design approach that has revolutionized our experience with applications. This model prioritizes a seamless user experience (UX), ensuring the applications work perfectly even when the internet is down or unreliable.

2.1. Why Offline-First?

Traditionally, developers used to work on an 'Online-First' approach, where applications depended heavily on reliable and high-speed connectivity to function properly. As we transitioned to a mobile-first world, this model started showing its shortcomings. Connectivity is not always consistent - sometimes it's slow, other times unavailable. Moreover, data usage also became another crucial factor to consider. Consequently, the approach evolved to a new paradigm, which prioritized a seamless user experience, irrespective of internet connectivity - The 'Offline-First' Approach.

The Offline-First Approach effectively transcends the constraint of network availability. It stores local versions of data, enabling users to continue their tasks as if they were online. When the connection is reinstated, it synchronizes with the online servers, updating any changes made. This revolutionary approach ensures a powerful, uninterrupted, user experience.

2.2. Designing Offline-First Applications

1. **Identifying Offline Scenarios:** The first step to designing an

Offline-First application is comprehending the possible scenarios in which your application could be used offline. This could range from a momentary lapse in connectivity to prolonged periods of disconnection.

2. **Determining Essential Features:** Once you've identified your offline scenarios, you need to discern the application's essential features. Which elements of your application would remain functional offline, and which wouldn't?

3. **Providing Feedback:** Offline usage shouldn't confuse the user, but rather provide seamless transparency. Users need to be regularly updated about their connection status and data synchronization updates.

4. **Data Synchronization:** The application needs to be capable of storing changes made offline and updating them once the connection is restored, ensuring seamless service delivery.

Applications following the Offline-First Approach aren't just built for the offline experience. They are designed to provide an uninterrupted experience, regardless of online status or fluctuating network conditions.

2.3. Data Synchronization in Offline-First Applications

A major challenge with Offline-First Applications is synchronizing the offline changes to the server when the connection is restored. This demands a smart-sync strategy:

1. **Conflict Resolution:** Require a strategy to resolve conflicts when changes are made to the same data block simultaneously offline and online. Timestamps or vector clocks can help distinguish simultaneous changes, but the real challenge lies in resolving them.

3

2. **Prioritizing Data Sync:** Not all data holds the same importance. Having a priority policy further helps in managing data syncing when the connection is reinstated.

3. **Bi-directional Syncing:** Changes could be initiated both on the client or server side. Your application needs a bidirectional syncing system to manage these changes.

4. **Partitioning Data:** It's wise to categorize data based on its relevance to the user. This helps in optimizing the amount of data stored locally.

Synchronizing data is a pressing issue in Offline-First Applications. It requires careful planning and management to ensure data consistency and automatic updates once the connection is reinstated.

2.4. Deployment of Offline-First Applications

Deployment is the ultimate step of this journey where all the building blocks are finally put together to create the application. Applications that inherently follow an offline-first approach can benefit from service workers, a powerful tool that plays a significant role in caching and network requests.

Conclusion

The world isn't entirely online yet. And until it is, Offline-First Approach will prevail as the optimal way in ensuring continuous, reliable service to users. Consequently, understanding, designing, deploying, and managing an Offline-First Application has become a critical skill in the modern era. With our constant digital evolution, no doubt this trend is here to stay. And with proper understanding and handling, it not only creates a great user experience but also unravels new possibilities in the digital world.

Chapter 3. The Mechanics of Synchronization

Synchronization, in the context of offline-first applications, refers to the process of ensuring application data is up-to-date across multiple devices and/or platforms no matter the internet connectivity status. This mechanism is pivotal to seamless user experience as it allows for uninterrupted work and usage, regardless of network conditions.

3.1. A Deep Dive into Data Synchronization

To understand the mechanics of synchronization in an effective manner, it is crucial to delve a bit deeper into the concept of data synchronization. At its core, data synchronization is a process that ensures consistency among data from a source to a target data storage and vice versa. It essentially establishes a common state of data across different platforms and devices.

Successful data synchronization should meet certain requirements. Notably, it should be bidirectional where changes made in one device are reflected in others. It should also consider conflict resolutions, where the system resolves discrepancies between different changes made to the same data simultaneously.

3.2. Conflict Resolution

A central challenge of data synchronization is conflict resolution. When two different changes are made simultaneously on the same data from two different sources, it creates a conflict. Different systems use different algorithms for conflict resolution, based on the system requirements, but the most common methods include:

- "Last Write Wins": This method considers the change with the most recent timestamp as the most recent change.

- "First Write Wins": Here, the conflict is resolved in favor of the source which initiated the change first.

- "Custom Rules": Some systems use predefined business rules to resolve discrepancies.

While working with conflict resolutions, applications should be mindful of conflicts which can potentially repeat themselves, referred to as 'Update Loops.' This can be prevented by implementing version control.

3.3. Implementing Version Control

Implementing version control is essential for conflict resolution. It involves keeping track of different versions of data and ensuring the application-data interface always reflects the most recent and accurate version. This often takes the form of an automated system which oversees all data updates, following a strict set of rules defined by the developers.

To accomplish this, each change is assigned an incremental version number. This number helps systems and developers track changes and isolate conflicts. Additionally, it assists in rollbacks if needed, making it a crucial component of data synchronization.

3.4. Synchronization Models

There are primarily two types of synchronization models: manual syncing and automatic syncing.

1. Manual Syncing: In manual synchronization, the user triggers a sync operation. It starts when the user initiates a data-input operation and ends when the data is updated across all devices.

2. Automatic Syncing: In automatic synchronization, updates are propagated to all devices automatically by the system, often in real-time or near-real-time.

In selecting the appropriate synchronization model, one should consider factors such as the application's type, the infrastructure in place, and the nature of data.

3.5. The Role of APIs

APIs (Application Programming Interfaces) are critical in maintaining synchronization in offline-first applications. They govern the interaction between different parts of an application and enable the communication of data, especially during data synchronization. APIs allow for data exchange even when a device is offline, storing changes that are then propagated to other devices once connectivity is re-established.

3.6. Offline First Synchronization

At its essence, an offline-first approach means treating network connectivity as an enhancement, not a requirement. Synchronization, in this context, requires a blend of technologies and tactics to ensure a consistent and seamless user experience.

Typically, an offline-first application will use service workers, a type of web worker. These are run in the background, separate from the webpage, enabling the application to work offline and in low-connectivity scenarios. They are installed during the first interaction and remain even after users close the page, ensuring seamless synchronization when the connection is restored.

3.7. A Look at Mobile Synchronization Strategies

Given the major role that mobile devices play in our lives, it is worth delving into some of the strategies employed in mobile offline-first applications:

1. Preemptive Data Caching: This involves storing data on local databases for offline use. This can be done predictively, based on usage patterns, or selectively, based on user preference.

2. Background Synchronization: This refers to the process of updating application state and local databases while the application is not in use. The goal is to always present users with an up-to-date view of the application upon launch.

Offline-first synchronization strategy is, therefore, a mission-critical part of application design that ensures seamless service delivery, irrespective of connectivity issues. Ultimately, it is a core facet of modern applications that warrants focused study and strategic implementation.

Chapter 4. Diving into Offline Data Storage

In the realm of offline-first applications, one cannot dismiss the paramount value of offline data storage. This is the linchpin upon which the application's functionality hinges even in the absence or inconsistency of connectivity. Navigating this aspect combines an understanding of essential strategies with the selection of apt technologies for efficient storage and retrieval of data.

4.1. Understanding Data Storage Strategies

A suitable offline data storage strategy is at the heart of building an efficient offline-first application. It neccessitates a keen consideration of the required data, how the data changes, and how frequently the users need to interact. In drawing up a strategy, one must contend with two key types of storage: local storage and IndexedDB.

Local storage, a type of web storage, provides the advantage of simplicity. It's like a permanent cookies store for your web application, keeping basic data types such as strings and numbers. However, it's limited in its capacity and lacks the functionality to deal with more complex data types.

The IndexedDB, on the other hand, is a low-level API for client-side storage, designed to manage significant amounts of structured data, including files and blobs. It provides rich query capabilities, and its transactions feature ensures data integrity even if a tab is closed throughout a transaction.

4.2. Local Storage and Its Techniques

Operation of local storage revolves around four critical methods: setItem for adding new data, getItem for data retrieval, removeItem for data deletion, and clear for wiping the entire storage. Key/value pairs form the basis for data storage with this method.

Take note though, local storage isn't designed to handle sensitive data. Browser vulnerabilities or XSS attacks can expose data stored in local storage. Thus, if an application deals with sensitive data like user authentication information, it's advisable to choose a more secure storage option.

4.3. IndexedDB and Its Intricacies

For offline-first applications that handle a large and complex set of data, IndexedDB offers a much more robust alternative to local storage. Handling IndexedDB is more complex, but offers greater rewards. Unlike local storage, IndexedDB supports transactions: which allow multiple read/write operations, guaranteeing that they either all succeed or all fail. This ensures data consistency.

Another distinguishing feature of IndexedDB is that it works asynchronously to prevent any blockage in the application's user interface. That means, the user interface is responsive even when sizable amounts of data are being read or written.

4.4. Selection of Right Tools

Essential to developing a seamless offline-first application is the choice of the right tools for data storage. Some popular libraries and tools used include PouchDB, localForage, and Dexie.

PouchDB's strength lies in its ability to replicate data between PouchDB and CouchDB instances, making it perfect for apps requiring data synchronization. LocalForage provides a simple developer interface, allowing developers to store various data types like blobs, strings, numbers without having to deal with encoding and decoding them. Dexie simplifies IndexedDB with its intuitive API, mitigating much of IndexedDB's complexity.

4.5. Future of Offline Data Storage

Despite the immense progress in offline data storage, technology is an ever-evolving landscape. Innovations like Service Workers, which function as a network proxy, controlling the web page requests directly, are increasingly significant. Moreover, intriguing progress is already underway with WebAssembly, enabling an application to run at near-native speeds, thereby creating possibilities to write data-intensive applications in the browser.

In conclusion, offline data storage has never been more vital. A thorough understanding of its strategies, tools, and future trends is indispensable for anyone wanting to build or even understand offline-first applications. It's about combining prudent strategy with booming technology, rendering the application performant regardless of the connectivity.

Chapter 5. Optimizing User Experience during Network Disruptions

Network disruptions tend to be among the most frustrating experiences for users, leading to disengagement and potential loss of customers. Fortunately, optimizing for offline-first applications can significantly reduce these odds. The following sections offer an expansive understanding of the concept, its strategic importance, key components, technical considerations, and practical techniques to optimize user experience during network disruptions.

5.1. Understanding Network Disruptions

Network disruptions occur when online services become inaccessible to users due to various factors, typically related to the internet connection. Numerous factors can cause disruptions, including a weak signal, overloaded network, or outright loss of connectivity. Users often face decreased app performance, slow loading times, or inability to access services altogether, leading to a harsh degradation of their experience. By redesigning your strategy around the use of offline-first applications, you can combat these problems effectively and assure a seamless user experience.

5.2. The Relevance of Offline-first Applications

Offline-first applications have their data and functionality largely resident on the device itself, rendering them capable of normal operations even when an internet connection is feeble or non-existent. They store data locally and sync with servers when connectivity is robust, allowing users to interact with the app regardless of network quality. Given today's global reliance on mobile devices amid varying network infrastructures, offline-first applications can significantly enhance user experience while also widening the potential market, reaching regions with spotty or unreliable internet access.

5.3. Offline/Online Data Syncing

A key feature of offline-first applications is their ability to sync data. This is accomplished using a robust synchronization mechanism that instantly saves changes made offline to the local data store. Once a stable internet connection is present, these changes are then synced with the online server. A robust syncing system must handle potential conflicts arising from multiple users altering the same piece of data in different offline states.

5.4. Caching and Prefetching: Key Strategies

Among the offline optimization techniques, two are particularly noteworthy - caching and prefetching. Caching involves storing data retrieved from servers, thus reducing load times on subsequent requests. Prefetching, on the other hand, involves loading and locally storing data that the user will likely need, based on analyzed browsing patterns. These two techniques can significantly reduce the impact of network disruptions and enhance user experience.

5.5. UX Design for Offline-first Apps

One crucial aspect to consider while designing offline-first applications is the user experience (UX). Like any other application, offline-first apps should be designed with the user's needs and expectations in mind. A key feature of a well-designed offline-first app is seamless transitioning between online and offline states with minimal user intervention, along with clear indicators of current connectivity status and data synchronization.

5.6. Bridging the User Perception Gap

Taking into account the "perception gap," i.e., the difference between the actual and perceived performance of an application, is important. A well-designed offline-first application can help bridge this gap by ensuring consistent performance regardless of network conditions, leading to improved user perceptions. Techniques such as providing immediate feedback to user actions, graceful degradation, and offering offline-friendly features can considerably fill this gap.

5.7. Offline-First and Mobile First: A Synergy

The overlap between offline-first and mobile-first design paradigms is notable. Both emphasize the performance, availability, and user experience over diverse network conditions, making them a great duo in optimizing network resilience. Offline-first makes your app reliable in times of network disruptions, whereas mobile-first optimizes for differing screen sizes, internet speeds, and usage patterns.

5.8. Conclusion

In conclusion, optimizing user experience during network disruptions and designing responsive, reliable offline-first applications go hand in hand. Understanding the technical underpinnings, as well as the UX design principles for offline capability is a paramount consideration for there to be successful application performance. Understanding how caching, prefetching, and efficient data syncing translate to an improved user experience is essential, alongside aptly addressing user perception gaps. The marriage of offline-first and mobile-first can further bolster the overall performance, making your app adaptable to an array of environments and usage contexts. The optimization journey may seem daunting but taking it one step at a time will result in significant strides to user satisfaction.

Chapter 6. Effective Strategies for Data Consistency

In this digital era, application performance governs the acceptance and popularity of an application. Effective data synchronization is a critical component in maintaining seamless user interactions, especially in Offline-First Applications. Offline-first applications aim to provide an uninterruptible user experience, regardless of the efficiency of overall network connectivity, by storing data locally and synchronizing with the server when a connection becomes available. This approach inevitably thrusts data consistency issues to the center stage.

An effective data consistency strategy is cardinal for the success of such applications. However, without technical insights, data consistency can be an elusive concept to many. This exploration will help bridge that gap by laying out detailed strategies essential for ensuring data consistency in Offline-First Applications.

6.1. Understanding the Concept of Data Consistency

Data consistency in the domain of applications ensures that the user sees the same data, regardless of any middle-layer alterations due to network connectivity status, simultaneous updates, or other related factors. Achieving data consistency is a journey filled with challenges, considering our focus on Offline-First Applications are persistently prone to connection interruptions and irregularities.

In systems where data change is a continuum, achieving absolute consistency requires a trade-off with the application's availability and partition-tolerance, as given by the CAP theorem. This, combined with the potential for conflicts while syncing changes, brings data consistency to the fore as a critical area to handle.

6.2. Eventual Consistency in Offline-First Applications

One popular approach is to adopt an eventual consistency model, a relaxed version where discrepancies in the data due to updates are allowed for a brief while until the system eventually becomes consistent.

In Offline-First Applications, a well-implemented eventual consistency model can lead to improved user experience as it allows continuous interactions even during offline periods, banking on the assurance that data will sync when connectivity is restored. However, managing this temporary period when concurrent data versions co-exist can be challenging.

6.3. Conflict Resolution

Conflicts can occur any time the application is reconciling multiple versions of data, often stemming from simultaneous updates on different devices. While several strategies exist for conflict resolution, the context of your application should dictate the option you choose. It could be either 'Client Wins', where the client's change overrides others, or 'Server Wins', where the server has the final say.

However, these are too simplistic for most real-world applications. More adaptive strategies include 'Record-level Merge', where the latest change for each data record is chosen, and 'Field-level Merge', where the change level gets down to individual data fields.

6.4. Offline Data Capture and Latency

Capturing data changes while offline is vital. The local storage should be designed to effectively store and mark data changes for sync whenever connectivity is available. Additionally, the data sync latency has to be managed effectively to ensure the user experiences data consistency. This could be managed by a well-designed sync protocol which prioritizes the more crucial data for synchronization.

6.5. Implementation Strategies

While we have described the theoretical aspects, the implementation of these strategies will depend on myriad factors such as the features of the application, offline availability requirements, nature of data interactions, etc. The eventual goal should be to implement these strategies in such a way that the application optimizes its performance without sacrificing data consistency or user experience.

6.6. Leveraging Existing Solutions

There are multiple high-profile data synchronization services and libraries available such as CouchDB, Firebase, and Realm; they provide support for data synchronization with built-in conflict resolution strategies. Investing time to understand how these tools manage data consistency can provide insights into the practical aspects and help you to design a more efficient application.

6.7. Lessons from Leaders

Studying the approaches taken by successful offline-first applications can provide very useful insights. Notable applications such as Evernote and Google Docs have made notable strides in offline data management and synchronization.

In conclusion, developing an effective data consistency strategy for Offline-First Applications requires a solid understanding of the challenges and a smart choice of conflict resolution strategies, combined with an efficient synchronization protocol. With such a strategy in place, you are ready to empower your application users with seamless, consistent interactions, whether they are online or offline.

Chapter 7. Caching Mechanisms and Offline-First Applications

In an era of ubiquitous online presence, the ability to use apps effectively when network connection is poor or even non-existent is becoming increasingly critical. This where Offline-first applications enter the scene, equipped with caching mechanisms to render data and resources accessible regardless of network connectivity status.

7.1. Understanding Caching

Before delving deep into the role of caching in offline-first applications, it is critical to understand what caching is. In simple terms, caching is a process of storing data temporarily in a fast access hardware component called cache. In the context of applications, cache is a software component that saves data so that future requests for the same data can be served faster.

Caching owes its effectiveness to its capacity to serve repeated requests quicker by reducing latency and helping applications scale in the face of mounting demands. It works in congruence with principles such as locality of reference – spatial and temporal, thus boosting application performance significantly.

Without caching, applications would begin each operation from scratch, causing substantial delays and sacrificing the user experience. As such, caching acts as an enabler for providing a seamless user experience, ensuring performance isn't compromised when an application needs to fetch or save data, often on distant servers.

7.2. Caching Mechanisms

There are several mechanisms available for caching data within an application. Understanding the distinctions amongst them is fundamental to capitalizing on their potential within offline-first applications.

7.2.1. 1. Local Cache

Applications often store cache data directly on the device where they are installed. This method, known as local caching, can range from simple key-value storage mechanisms to more complex relational databases. These local databases, such as SQLite and Realm, allow you to cache data that your app might need offline.

Local cache tends to be the most straightforward option to implement. It allows developers to store a wide variety of data on the device, including text, images, videos, and even sizable binary files. However, it should be judiciously as too much data can overwhelm storage and slow operations.

7.2.2. 2. Server Cache

In contrast to local cache, server cache is stored on the server that an application interacts with. This kind of storage allows the server to provide responses to user requests from cache, significantly reducing response times, as the server may not need to fetch data from its database or compute a complex response.

While this mechanism falls short of providing offline access to data, it amplifies the overall user experience by improving application performance during online operation.

7.2.3. 3. Distributed Cache

Here, cache is stored across a system of interconnected nodes, and it grants benefits of both local and server cache. Not only does it reduce latency by keeping cache close to its application(s), but it also goes beyond the limitations of a single machine's memory capacity by enabling horizontal scaling.

7.3. Integrating Caching in Offline-First Applications

To institute offline-first apps, developers require an effective synchronization module, but they also require a precise mechanism to cache data locally. This combination allows applications to operate seamlessly even when offline, providing a superior user experience.

7.3.1. Choosing the Right Caching Strategy

It is essential to find the right caching strategy that accommodates the requirements of both the application and its intended user base. A well-chosen caching strategy assists offline capability by providing stale or older cached data when the network is unavailable, while ensuring that the updated data is always the first option when available.

Several strategies might be applied:

Mirroring Strategy: The simplest method, in which every bit of online data is replicated and stored on the device itself. This strategy is effective when data is not significantly large, and where maintaining an exact data replica isn't a concern for storage.

Selective Strategy: In situations where discs space is an issue or where network availability is generally reliable, a selective strategy may be employed. In this approach, only a subset of data considered as high-priority (based on the user's activity pattern, for instance) is stored offline for later use.

Incremental Strategy: This strategy includes saving only the changes that have been made to data since the last online session.

7.3.2. Implementing Caching in Offline-First Applications

Several tools and techniques can expedite the process of integrating caching into the architecture of offline-first applications.

Service Workers are becoming the mainstay for offline-first applications. They are scripts that your browser runs in the background, facilitating features such as push notifications and background syncs. In terms of caching, service workers can intercept network requests, manage cache and serve cached responses.

IndexedDB is another option, allowing developers to store data in the browser, importantly supporting significant amounts of concurrent data.

When developing mobile applications, developers might utilize SQLite (for Android) or Core Data (for iOS) for caching.

In conclusion, integrating effective caching mechanisms in offline-first applications offers undeniable advantages by ensuring seamless usage irrespective of connection status. By adopting an appropriate caching strategy and its right implementation, offline-first applications can elevate the user experience significantly, encouraging user retention and building robust, usable, and resilient applications.

Chapter 8. Scaling and Performance: Key Considerations

With the increasing prominence of offline-first applications in today's dynamic and interconnected digital environment, a meticulous attention to scaling and performance is essential. This chapter casts an in-depth look into different dimensions associated with scaling these solutions and optimizing their performance, enhancing user experience even in the face of connectivity hitches.

8.1. Understanding the Performance Essentials

The crux of any offline-first application's success lies in its functionality, particularly its effectiveness during offline scenarios. A key component to that is identifying the typical performance requirements for such an application.

To start, consider an application's relative demand on system resources, specifically storage and processing power. The application should be designed with efficient code to ensure lower resource usage, allowing the application to perform optimally even on devices with limited capacity.

Given that offline applications heavily rely on storing data locally, the issue of storage optimization is paramount. Efficacy of storage allocation, data retrieval, and efficient data synchronization mechanisms will be integral to consider.

8.2. Data Synchronization and Its Impact on Performance

Data synchronization is at the core of offline-first applications. However, this very process can become a performance bottleneck, impeding the application's overall functionality. Accordingly, developers need to consider the following factors:

- The frequency of synchronization: The more frequent the synchronization, the more the system resource demand, leading to performance issues.

- Network conditions: While the application might mainly be used offline, network conditions during synchronization times can significantly impact performance.

- Data complexity: The complexity of data to be synchronized also influences the application's performance.

- Conflict resolution strategy: Having an efficient strategy to handle data conflicts during synchronization is key to maintaining performance.

8.3. Latency and Performance Constraints

Latency is another important factor to consider. Offline applications are typically used in environments where connectivity is inconsistent. High latency during operations like synchronization could negatively affect user experience.

In such instances, applications should be designed to put user experience at the forefront. This could involve implementing user feedback mechanisms during synchronization, or designing the app's user interface in a manner that masks latency - offering a perception of seamless operation even when offline.

8.4. Systemic Efficiency and Scaling Strategy

Implementing offline capabilities necessitates judicious use of system resources, especially memory, CPU, and battery. You also need to consider the future scalability of the application. As an application grows and user base expands, the systems supporting such growth should be robust enough to handle scaling efficiently.

Think about aspects like data partitioning, which help in effective data management when scaling. Monitor application usage and metrics to identify potential performance bottlenecks and remedy them proactively.

8.5. Optimizing for Multiple Platforms

Offline-first applications need to cater to more than one platform in most cases. Optimization efforts should therefore account for this diversity, targeting specific metrics and characteristics of each platform, be it Android, iOS, Windows, or web. Performance indicators might vary, and perfecting these across platforms is a good starting point.

8.6. The Path to Performance Testing

In order to gauge the effectiveness of an application's performance, testing is paramount. Performance testing goes beyond mere functionality checks – it dives deep into the application's underlying systems, assessing how effectively the application uses system resources, initiates data synchronization, and manages possible latency.

Use a mix of both physical devices and emulators for testing. Carry out load testing, stress testing, and endurance testing. Simulate various network conditions to understand how the application performs in diverse scenarios.

8.7. Strengthening Security without Compromising Performance

Security is a central concern, especially for offline-first applications given their data storage approach. However, security measures often come at a cost to system resources. Cryptographic workloads can have a significant CPU draw. Hence, considering performance while ensuring data security becomes critical.

Striking a performance-security balance involves a carefully charted combination of encryption techniques, data sanitization methods, and other security features, all optimized towards minimal system resource draw.

Summarily, the key to effective offline-first applications lies in the synergy between design, development, and deployment approaches. Its timely evolution helps in maintaining scalability and performance as per growing user needs and dynamics of the digital realm.

Chapter 9. Case Studies in Offline-First Solutions

In this thorough dive into offline-first solutions, we will look at some intriguing case studies that highlight this approach and detail the myriad of ways it has improved both application performance and user experience.

9.1. Ethical Compass App

One can't discuss offline-first solutions without mentioning the Ethical Compass, an application designed to assist humanitarian workers make critical decisions in difficult situations. The very nature of the locations and situations they work in means that this app must function flawlessly offline.

The developers faced many challenges, including the housing of complex decision trees, multimedia content, and additional resources within the application itself. By basing the application on a Service Worker, they ensured a seamless offline experience that carefully cached critical data without overwhelming device storage capacities.

With the help of IndexedDB, a low-level API for client-side storage of significant amounts of structured data, the developers could store and retrieve key-value pairs that even worked with high amounts of data, and complex threaded transactions weren't an issue. Web SQL, another important technology utilized, enabled the application with a small SQL database engine.

The efficiency and usability of the Ethical Compass have garnered accolades, clearly evidencing the robust potential of offline-first solutions in demanding circumstances.

9.2. The Everest Project

In a setting where connectivity borders on non-existence, the comprehensive offline-first approach adopted in The Everest Project, a massive scientific initiative, demonstrated how instrumental offline-first applications could be.

Data collection at high altitudes is a monumental task, with scarce internet connectivity. The offline-first data collection application, developed for this project, allowed scientists to collect and safely store pertinent data, even in the absence of internet connectivity.

The application leveraged PouchDB, an open-source JavaScript database designed to run within a browser. It enabled the scientists to store data offline and synchronize it later when an internet connection became available. The app's synchronization concept, commonly known as "data replication," involves copying and maintaining database objects in multiple databases belonging to a distributed system.

PouchDB helped manage conflicts and ensure data integrity during the synchronization phase, proving to be an exceptional tool for offline data collection and syncing. The Everest Project sets a benchmark for the implementation of offline-first strategies in challenging environments.

9.3. HealthWorker App

HealthWorker, an application developed for healthcare workers in remote parts of the world, is another innovative example of an offline-first application. Reliant on a PWA (Progressive Web App) architecture, this application provides a comprehensive health record system that operates effectively in areas with limited or no internet access.

HealthWorker uses IndexedDB for storage and Service Worker for caching, while Web Workers handle resource-intensive tasks in the background. As the data is stored on users' devices until a network connection is detectable, IndexedDB and its handling of arbitrary amounts of structured data come into play significantly. Service Worker ensures speedy content load time during both offline and liminal connectivity periods.

The application also makes use of Background Sync API, which allows data to be queued when offline and then be shared once the device is online again, ensuring an uninterrupted user experience and guaranteeing that no data is lost during transmission. The success of the HealthWorker app is a testament to the depth to which offline-first strategies can be woven into the fabric of an application's architecture to deliver essential services against all odds.

The case studies mentioned showcase the potential and versatility of offline-first solutions across a diverse range of domains and scenarios, demonstrating the viability of offline-first applications even in the most challenging environments. As our reliance on digital solutions continues to grow, understanding and implementing these strategies becomes more critical. The future of applications lies in offline-first solutions that deliver superior performance, anytime, anywhere.

Chapter 10. Offline-First in Mobile and Web Applications

The term 'Offline-First' is becoming increasingly commonplace in the sphere of digital design and application development. A paradigm shift from the traditional online-always frameworks, Offline-First concepts prioritize effective functioning even when network connectivity is sporadic or altogether absent. This chapter provides a comprehensive overview of the Offline-First stance in the design, development, and deployment of mobile and web applications.

10.1. Understanding Offline-First

Offline-First does not explicitly imply that applications are geared toward complete offline usage. Instead, it embodies the philosophy that applications should provide a seamless user experience irrespective of network strength or availability. This means that in areas of limited connectivity, instead of stalling, Offline-First applications continue to function while granting users access to interact with certain features and data.

This paradigm emerged as a response to the significant challenges posed by traditional applications, which upon losing connectivity, would often become completely unresponsive, usually leaving the users either waiting for service restoration or experiencing substantial loss of unsaved work.

Offline-First applications feature innovative layers of design and architecture to ensure robustness despite network inconsistencies. This approach certainly does not aim to eliminate online functionality; instead, it seeks to enhance resilience against disruptions, often resulting from a weak or unstable internet connection.

10.2. Designing Offline-First Applications

The design aspect of Offline-First applications plays a critical role in ensuring a smooth and efficient user experience. One of the key design principles behind an Offline-First app is the use of a local data store.

1. Local Data Store: All data required for the application to run should be stored on the device. This includes not only user-specific data but also any structural data or metadata needed for the application to function properly.

The challenge here lies in deciding which data should be saved locally. All data cannot be stored due to device storage limitations, and it's important to determine the most crucial and frequently accessed data.

1. Usability: While designing an Offline-First application, the user's application interaction should be taken into consideration. Any functionality that requires an active internet connection should be indicated clearly to the user to prevent any confusion or frustration when the app is used offline.

10.3. Developing Offline-First Applications

In this realm, modern technologies help developers integrate Offline-First principles with relative ease.

1. Service Workers: Service workers are one of the more modern solutions to implementing offline functionality. Written in JavaScript, they play a crucial mediator role between web pages and network resources. This significantly contributes to caching

and thereby facilitates offline functionality.

2. Local Databases: Technologies such as IndexedDB and WebSQL enable the storage of sizable amounts of data on the local user's device.

3. Caching Mechanisms: Application Cache (AppCache), though increasingly considered deprecated, has been a significant contributor to offline functionality. Developers are encouraged to migrate to Service Workers and the Cache API, permitting more granular resource control.

10.4. Deploying and Testing Offline-First Applications

A well-designed and appropriately developed Offline-First app also needs to be effectively tested and deployed to ensure it functions as expected in different scenarios.

1. Testing: There is a strong need for thorough testing to ensure that the app behaves correctly when there is interrupted or no connectivity. Tests should involve various scenarios including intermittent connectivity, no connectivity, and recovery after reconnection.

2. Deployment: Deployment of such applications should be able to cater to various updates, including those related to data, without disrupting the user experience.

10.5. The Synchronized Data Challenge

Perhaps the most sensitive aspect of Offline-First applications exists in the necessity for efficient synchronization. Achieving harmony between local and server data once the device regains connectivity is essential. This is particularly challenging when there are multiple users, conflicting updates, or differing versions of the same data.

10.6. Advantages of Offline-First Applications

Offline-First apps offer several advantages, including:

1. Seamless User Experience: Users can continue to interact with the app, even when network connectivity is weak or unavailable.

2. Increased Engagement: By ensuring apps remain functional despite connectivity issues, user engagement is likely to be consistently higher.

3. Flexibility: It offers flexibility to users, allowing them to use the application anytime, anywhere.

In a world increasingly running on digital applications, the Offline-First approach appears more relevant than ever. By ensuring uninterrupted app functioning, it aids in maintaining user engagement, thereby laying the foundation for a new era in app design, development, and experience.

Chapter 11. The Future of Offline-First Applications

In the wake of rapid technological evolution, Offline-First Applications have begun to stake their claim in the landscape of digital innovation. These applications, by design, prioritize effective operation in the absence of network connectivity, ensuring reliable service delivery.

This approach is quite the departure from conventional application designs where connectivity is presumed. It is transforming the digital space, bringing forth a perspective shift on what responsive application design should entail. The following sections further delve into this significant paradigm shift, assessing potential trends, and predicting the future of Offline-First Applications.

11.1. The Technological Evolution of Offline-First Applications

From the early stages, Offline-First Applications were built to work primarily in challenging scenarios without internet, making use of available technologies to provide a seamless experience. As technology evolved, these applications followed suit, leveraging advancements such as service workers and IndexedDB for improved performance.

Going forward, we can expect this trajectory to continue- with even more advanced technologies stepping in to push the envelope further. The rise of Edge computing, for instance, has vast implications for Offline-First Applications. With computing and storage moving closer to the edge, these applications have the potential to operate with less dependence on the cloud, reducing latency and further enhancing the user experience.

Machine learning and artificial intelligence, likewise, hold great promise. Offline-First Applications could leverage these technologies to derive more intelligent insights into user behavior, enabling them to make more informed decisions about data storage and retrieval.

11.2. The User Experience Revolution

One of the fundamental principles of Offline-First Applications is a seamless user experience, irrespective of network conditions. This commitment to consistent user experience has led to an outpouring of creative designs and innovative solutions from application developers worldwide.

In the future, this focus on user experience will be more front and center than ever before. As users increasingly expect on-demand services, the tolerance for outages and lags will diminish. Therefore, achieving a smooth, uninterrupted user interface with Offline-First Applications will become not just a 'good-to-have' feature but a critical factor in service delivery.

11.3. The Business Implications

Offline-First Applications aren't just about enhancing the user experience or leveraging advanced technology; they also offer substantial business benefits. For businesses operating in regions with limited connectivity, these applications enable them to reach untapped markets, providing services in areas previously thought inaccessible.

As we move forward, brands and businesses might consider Offline-First Applications as a key strategy in their expansion plans. In a digital age where constant connectivity can't be assured universally, applications that can function effectively under such limitations carry a significant competitive advantage. More companies are likely to invest in these applications, not just as a failsafe against unpredictable and unstable network conditions but as a proactive measure to access a wider demographic.

11.4. The Social Impact

The potential social impact of Offline-First Applications extends beyond the realm of business. In the grand scheme of things, these applications can become tools for digital inclusion, reaching individuals or communities who typically have limited access to online services due to network restrictions.

Imagine the impact when educational apps continue to function offline, enabling students in remote areas to learn at their pace. Or healthcare apps providing essential follow-up instructions and medication reminders even in a connectivity blackout.

As we look ahead, Offline-First Applications hold the potential to bridge digital divide, ensuring that the advantages of the digital world reach far and wide, irrespective of network limitations.

11.5. Conclusion: A World Not So Dependent on Connectivity

The advent of Offline-First Applications presents an interesting paradox. On one hand, we are engineering breakthrough technologies and fostering unprecedented connectivity. Yet, at the same time, we are developing applications designed to function effectively without this connectivity.

It's here that the true beauty of Offline-First Applications emerges. As the world ventures forth into an increasingly digital future, these applications serve to remind us that everyone should be part of this journey. Whether a user faces limited network accessibility or none at all, Offline-First Applications promise to deliver a seamless user experience.

Future developments in this arena are likely to emphasize inclusivity, accessibility, and user experience, paving the way for a digital world that isn't solely dependent on connectivity but thrives in its presence and absence alike.